MW00957915

Bunkei: Japanese Sentence Patterns for JLPT N5:

Master the Japanese Language Proficiency Test N5

Clay & Yumi Boutwell

INTRODUCTION

Taking the Japanese Language Proficiency Test is a great way to not only assess your Japanese skills, but also to give yourself a concrete goal for your studies.

Goals help increase motivation and motivation almost always results in progress. Also, by making plans to sit in a test (usually) in a different city, you are making an investment of time and money. There are few pressures in life that can motivate more than time or money. That's why I always recommend signing up and studying for the JLPT for any serious student of Japanese.

HOW TO USE THIS BOOK

This book offers a way to practice grammar, vocabulary, and reading using JLPT N5 level grammatical patterns in various example sentences. For each grammatical pattern, we'll switch out words and point out construction rules to give you a full understanding how to use that form.

We will present most examples in the polite *masu/desu* form. While other less polite forms may be, in some cases, more common, we think beginners should stick with the *masu/desu* form.

We highly recommend reading each example sentence several times—even dozens of times. Learning isolated vocabulary may be useful, but learning vocabulary within a natural context (sentence or phrase) while absorbing how the grammar is more efficient.

While you read (paperback, tablet, or computer), you may want to use your smartphone to play the sound files.

We assume you are using a textbook for your regular studies and have some (if only a touch) familiarity with very basic Japanese grammar. If not, we highly recommend getting a textbook to keep your learning structured before proceeding with this book. At the very minimum, to use this book, you must have a solid knowledge of hiragana.

SOUND FILES

While you read an example sentence (many times), listen to it. This will help with memorization. We also recommend "shadowing" the text. Listen to the Japanese and then repeat it out loud. Pay attention to the pronunciation and intonation.

The download link at the end of this book includes MP3s for all the grammar points and their example sentences.

The naming convention for the sound files is as follows:

- Grammar point: number [example: 1.mp3]

- Examples in the About section: number - AB [example: 3 -AB 1.mp3]

- Example sentences: number -EX 1 [example: 4 -EX 1.mp3]

ABOUT CLAY & YUMI

Yumi was a popular radio DJ in Japan for over ten years. She has extensive training in standard Japanese pronunciation which makes her perfect for creating these language instructional audio files.

Clay has been a passionate learner of Japanese for over twenty years now. He started what became his free language learning website, www.TheJapanesePage.com, way back in 1999 as a sort of diary of what he was learning.

In 2002, he and Yumi began TheJapanShop.com as a way to help students of Japanese get hard-to-find Japanese books. Since then, they have written dozens of books on various Japanese language topics.

--

Yumi and I are **very grateful** for your purchase and we truly hope this book will help you improve your Japanese. **We love our customers and don't take a single one of you for granted.** If you have any questions about this book or Japanese in general, I invite you to contact us below by email or on social media.

Clay & Yumi Boutwell (and Makoto & Megumi)
clay@thejapanshop.com

@theJapanShop
https://www.facebook.com/LearningJapaneseatTheJapanShop

http://www.TheJapanShop.com
https://www.MakotoPlus.com

CONTENTS

Contents

Let's Get Started!

Each lesson will begin with a discussion about the meaning or function of the grammatical pattern.

Then, we'll list three sentences in Japanese (but with furigana). Try to read and figure out the meaning before proceeding. Don't worry if you can't, but at least read each sentence (out loud if possible) several times.

Next, we'll look at each of the examples one-by-one and fully explain and define the words.

Lastly, we'll leave you with a few practice questions. These are plug and play sentences. You should, by this point, understand the 文型, the sentence pattern. Simply plug in the words in the correct order. If you need help, there will be hint section for the word order and a vocabulary list to refer to. The answers are at the bottom of the page. Please note, there may be multiple "correct" answers. Also, the actual test won't have this section, so don't become discouraged if this section is hard for you.

がんばりましょう！

1. は〜が

ABOUT:

■ The は topic particle with the が subject (sometimes object) marker is one of the most common sentence patterns in Japanese.

■ AはBがC。

In this construction, C tells us something about B and B tells us something about A, since A is the overall topic.

EXAMPLES:

1. 私の兄は、背が高いです。

2. 日本は、地震が多い国です。

3. 富士山は高さが３７７６メートルです。

EXAMPLE 1

<ruby>私<rt>わたし</rt></ruby> の <ruby>兄<rt>あに</rt></ruby>は、<ruby>背<rt>せ</rt></ruby>が<ruby>高<rt>たか</rt></ruby>いです。

[my | older brother (A) | as for (topic) | height (B) | tall (C) | is]

My older brother is tall.

[C (tall) tells us about the state of B (height) and B (height) tells us something about A (brother)]

EXAMPLE 2

<ruby>日本<rt>にほん</rt></ruby>は、<ruby>地震<rt>じしん</rt></ruby>が<ruby>多<rt>おお</rt></ruby>い<ruby>国<rt>くに</rt></ruby>です。

[lit. **As for** Japan (A) | earthquakes (B) | country with many (C) | is]

Japan is a country with many earthquakes.

EXAMPLE 3

<ruby>富士山<rt>ふじさん</rt></ruby>は、<ruby>高<rt>たか</rt></ruby>さが３７７６メートルです。

[Mt. Fuji | as for | height | 3776 meters | is]

Mt. Fuji is 3776 meters tall.

MAIN POINTS:

■ は almost always comes first

■ は is usually dropped once the listener knows what the topic is.

PRACTICE:

Using this form, how do you translate the following?
1) The elephant's nose is long.
2) Yumi is good at Japanese.

HINTS
1) elephant – は – nose – が – long

2) Yumi – は – Japanese – が – good at / skilled

Vocabulary:

ぞう elephant | はな nose | 長い long | 日本語 Japanese language | 上手 good at

ANSWERS:

1) ぞうは、はなが長い。

2) ゆみは、日本語が上手です。

2. ～があります

ABOUT:

■ There are / there is: This form shows existence (there is) or possession (I have). For inanimate objects (stationary objects, plants, etc), end the sentence with ～があります. For living things (people and animals), use ～がいます.

■ Casual form: がある

EXAMPLES:

1. 私の部屋には、机があります。

2. 森には、木があります。

3. 図書館には、本がたくさんあります。

EXAMPLE 1

私の部屋には、机があります。

[my | room | in | as for | desk | (ga) | exists]

There's a desk in my room.

In my room, there is a desk.

EXAMPLE 2

森には、木があります。

[forest | in | as for | tree | (ga) | exists]

There are trees in the forest.

EXAMPLE 3

図書館には、本がたくさんあります。

[library | in | as for | book | (ga) | many | exists]

There are many books in the library.

MAIN POINTS:

■ This corresponds to "to be" when dealing with

existence (there is, there are); use あります or います instead of です.

■ Inanimate objects use 〜があります

■ Animate objects use 〜がいます [the structure of the sentence is the same as with 〜があります]

PRACTICE:

Using this form, how do you translate the following?
1. There's a book on the table.
2. There's a supermarket next to the station.

HINTS
1. table – 's – above – on – book – there is

2. station – 's – next to – supermarket – there is

Vocabulary:

テーブル table | の of; 's [possessive; limits information: not just any top but the top of a table] | 上 above | に on; at | 本 book | 駅 (train) station | となり next to | スーパー supermarket

ANSWERS:

1. テーブルの上に、本があります。

2. 駅のとなりにスーパーがあります。

3. 〜ましょう

ABOUT:

■ *Let's*: An invitation. To suggest doing something with someone, use 〜ましょう

■ *The speaker's volition*: ましょう is also used to show a willingness to do something. Our example sentences illustrate the "let's" meaning, but ましょう can also mean "I will" (shows the speaker's volition) as in:

- 手を貸しましょうか。 Allow me to (I will) lend a hand.

- 私が彼に話しましょうか？ Shall I speak to him?

■ Construction: Using the *-masu* form of a verb, drop the ます and add ましょう.

EXAMPLES:

1. 駅<ruby>えき</ruby>に<u>行</u><ruby>い</ruby>きましょう。

2. 朝<ruby>あさ</ruby>ごはんを<u>食</u><ruby>た</ruby>べましょう。

3. 一緒<ruby>いっしょ</ruby>に学校<ruby>がっこう</ruby>に<u>行</u><ruby>い</ruby>きましょう。

EXAMPLE 1

駅<ruby>えき</ruby>に<u>行</u><ruby>い</ruby>きましょう。

[(train) station | to | let's go]

<u>Let's go</u> to the station.

EXAMPLE 2

朝<ruby>あさ</ruby>ごはんを<u>食</u><ruby>た</ruby>べましょう。

[breakfast | (direct object marker) | let's eat]

<u>Let's eat</u> breakfast.

EXAMPLE 3

<ruby>一緒<rt>いっしょ</rt></ruby>に<ruby>学校<rt>がっこう</rt></ruby>に<u><ruby>行<rt>い</rt></ruby>き</u>ましょう。

[together with | school | to | let's go]

<u>Let's go</u> to school together.

MAIN POINTS:

■ ましょう indicates an invitation or willingness of the speaker to do something. "Let's" or "allow me to…"

■ It asks the listener to accept the invitation or offer to do something.

PRACTICE:

Using this form, how do you translate the following?
1.   Let's go swimming from now.
2.   Let's change into our swimming trunks.

HINTS
1.   now | from | pool | at | let's swim

2.   swimwear | to | let's change

Vocabulary:

今<ruby>今<rt>いま</rt></ruby>から from now | プール pool | で at | 泳ぎましょ<ruby>泳<rt>およ</rt></ruby>う let's swim | 水着<ruby>水着<rt>みずぎ</rt></ruby> swimwear | に into | 着替<ruby>着替<rt>きが</rt></ruby>えまし ょう let's change

ANSWERS:

1. 今<ruby>今<rt>いま</rt></ruby>から、プールで泳<ruby>泳<rt>およ</rt></ruby>ぎましょう。

2. 水着<ruby>水着<rt>みずぎ</rt></ruby>に着替<ruby>着替<rt>きが</rt></ruby>えましょう。

4. 〜てもいいです（か）

ABOUT:

■ You may; may I?

■ This form is about giving or asking for permission to do something. It is a polite way to ask for permission with the か question marker. Or if you want to give someone permission to do something, you can make the て form of a verb and add いいです.

EXAMPLES:

1. となりに座_{すわ}ってもいいです（か？）

2. 質問_{しつもん}してもいいです（か？）

3. 薬_{くすり}を飲_のんでもいいです（か？）

EXAMPLE 1

となりに<ruby>座<rt>すわ</rt></ruby>ってもいいです（か？）

[next | to | sitting | would be good | (question)]

It's fine to sit next (to me) [without the か]

May I sit next (to you)? [with the か]

EXAMPLE 2

<ruby>質問<rt>しつもん</rt></ruby>してもいいです（か？）

[question | doing | would be good | (question)]

You may ask questions.

May I ask a question?

EXAMPLE 3

<ruby>薬<rt>くすり</rt></ruby>を<ruby>飲<rt>の</rt></ruby>んでもいいです（か？）

[medicine | (direct object marker) | drinking | would be
good | (question)]

It's fine to take the medicine.

May I take the medicine?

[Note: In Japanese, the verb 飲む (to drink) is used with medicine.]

MAIN POINTS:

■ 〜てもいいですか is a polite way to ask permission for something.

■ Drop the か to grant someone permission to do something.

PRACTICE:

Using this form, how do you translate the following?
1. May I eat my bento?
2. You may go home already.

HINTS
1. bento | を | eating | would be good | か

2. already | returning (home) | would be good

Vocabulary:

お弁当 bento; lunchbox | 食べて eating | もう already; now; by now | 帰って returning (home)

ANSWERS:

1. お弁当を食べてもいいですか？

2. もう帰ってもいいです。

5. 〜てはいけません

ABOUT:

■ must not; not allowed to

■ Used when something is prohibited or something ought not to be done.

EXAMPLES:

1. 図書館で大声で話してはいけません。

2. テストの間は、隣の人の答えを見てはいけません。

3. 甘いものを食べすぎてはいけません。

EXAMPLE 1

図書館で大声で話してはいけません。

[library | at | loud voice | with | speaking | must not]

You must not speak with a loud voice in the library.

EXAMPLE 2

テストの間^{あいだ}は、隣^{となり}の人^{ひと}の答^{こた}えを<u>見^みて</u>はいけません。

[test | of の (limits the information: duration **of** the test) | during | as for | neighboring person | 's | answer | (direct object marker) | seeing | not allowed]

During the test, you must not look at the paper of the person next to you.

EXAMPLE 3

甘^{あま}いものを<u>食^たべすぎて</u>はいけません。

[sweet | thing | (を direct object marker) | eating | too much | must not]

MAIN POINTS:

■ Used when something is prohibited or something ought not to be done.

PRACTICE:

Using this form, how do you translate the following?
1. Don't run at the pool.
2. You are not allowed to smoke in the restaurant.

HINTS
1. pool | at | は | running | must not

2. restaurant | at | tabacco | smoke (literally, suck) | must not

Vocabulary:

プール pool | では as for | 走^{はし}って running | レストラン restaurant | で at | たばこ tabacco; cigarettes | 吸^すって smoking; sucking

ANSWERS:

1. プールでは、走^{はし}ってはいけません。

2. レストランで、たばこを吸^すってはいけません。

6. 〜が好きです

ABOUT:

■ (I) like …

■ Simply add a noun (what you like), が, and then 好^すき
（です）

EXAMPLES:

1. 私^{わたし}の犬^{いぬ}は、<u>散歩^{さんぽ}</u>が好^すきです。

2. 私^{わたし}の兄^{あに}は、<u>動物^{どうぶつ}</u>が好^すきです。

3. 私^{わたし}は、<u>ラーメン</u>が好^すきです。

EXAMPLE 1

私^{わたし}の犬^{いぬ}は、<u>散歩^{さんぽ}</u>が好^すきです。

[my | dog | as for | go for walk | like (uses が)]

My dog likes to go on walks.

28

EXAMPLE 2

私 の 兄 は、動物 が 好き です。

[my | older brother | as for は | animals | likes]

My older brother likes animals.

EXAMPLE 3

私 は、ラーメン が 好き です。

[as for me, I | ramen | like]

I like ramen.

MAIN POINTS:

■ が is used with 好き.

PRACTICE:

Using this form, how do you translate the following?

1. She likes anime.
2. I like that movie.

HINTS

1. she | anime | like

2. your | matter/thing | like

Vocabulary:

彼女<ruby>かのじょ</ruby> she; her | アニメ anime | あの that (this form is used before nouns) | 映画<ruby>えいが</ruby> movie

ANSWERS:

1. 彼女は、アニメが好きです。

2. あの映画が好きです。

7. 〜ほうがいい

ABOUT:

■ It's better to (do ...)

■ Construction:

- plain past verb + ほうがいい

- noun + のほうがいい (often used with より for comparison – see the next, next grammar point)

EXAMPLES:

1. 野菜を食べたほうがいいです。

2. 休んだほうがいいです。

3. 大きな車のほうがいいです。

EXAMPLE 1

野菜を食べたほうがいいです。

[vegetables | を | eat | better]

It would be better to eat vegetables.

EXAMPLE 2

<ruby>休<rt>やす</rt></ruby>んだ**ほうがいいです**。

[rest | would be good]

It's best to rest.

EXAMPLE 3

<ruby>大<rt>おお</rt></ruby>きな <ruby>車<rt>くるま</rt></ruby> の**ほうがいいです**。

[big | car | is better]

A big car would be better.

MAIN POINTS:

■ Replace いい with any other adjective to mean "more
…": ほうがはやい faster than; ほうがひくい lower
than

PRACTICE:

Using this form, how do you translate the following?

1. It's better to go.
2. It's better to take medicine.

HINTS

1. gone | better to | です

2. medicine | を | drank | better to | です

Vocabulary:

行った went | ほうがいい better to | くすり
medicine | 飲んだ drank

ANSWERS:

1. 行ったほうがいいです

2. くすりを飲んだほうがいいです。

8. （なら）、～ほうがいい

ABOUT:

■ If (this) then (that) is better (to do)

■ Building from the previous construction, let's add a conditional comparison.

EXAMPLES:

1. 勉強するなら、図書館のほうがいいです。

2. 疲れたなら、家に帰って休んだほうがいい
   です。

3. 旅行に行くなら、海外のほうがいいです。

EXAMPLE 1

勉強するなら、図書館のほうがいいです。

[to study | if | library | better than]

If you are going to study, the library would be better.

EXAMPLE 2

疲れた**なら**、家に帰って休んだ**ほうがいいです**。

[tired | if | house | to | returning and | resting | would be good]

If you are tired, you should go back home and rest.

EXAMPLE 3

旅行に行く**なら**、海外の**ほうがいいです**。

[trip | on | to go | if | overseas | is better]

If you are going on a trip, overseas would be best.

MAIN POINTS:

■ This form makes the comparison conditional on some point.

PRACTICE:

Using this form, how do you translate the following?

1. If you are going to the supermarket, it is better

to go by car.

2. If you like anime, you should watch this.

HINTS

1. supermarket | to | go | if | car | by | went | better to | です

2. anime | が | like | if | this | を | saw | better to | です

Vocabulary:

スーパー supermarket | に to | 行く to go | なら if | 車 car | で by | 行った went | ほうがいい better to | アニメ anime | 好き like | これ this | 見た saw

ANSWERS:

1. スーパーに行くなら、車で行ったほうがいいです。

2. アニメが好きなら、これを見たほうがいいです。

9. 〜より〜ほうが

ABOUT:

■ more ... than ...

■ This construction compares two things. One is better, faster, more -er than the other.

EXAMPLES:

1. <u>ラーメン</u>より、<u>うどん</u>のほうが好きです。

2. <u>アニメ</u>より、<u>漫画</u>のほうが好きです。

3. 遊びに<u>行く</u>より、<u>家で寝ていた</u>ほうがいいです。

EXAMPLE 1

<u>ラーメン</u>より、<u>うどん</u>のほうが好きです。

[ramen | more than | udon | better | like]

I like udon more than ramen.

EXAMPLE 2

アニメより、漫画のほうが好きです。

[anime | more than | manga | better | like]

I like manga more than anime.

EXAMPLE 3

遊びに行くより、家で寝ていたほうがいいです。

[in order to play | to go | more than | house | at | slept | better]

Instead of going to play, it would be better to rest at home

MAIN POINTS:

■ The lesser of the two comes before より

PRACTICE:

Using this form, how do you translate the following?
1. The train would be cheaper than a taxi.
2. I like watching movies more than reading a book.

HINTS

1. taxi | more than | train | is cheaper

2. book | (direct object marker) | to read | more than | movie | (direct object marker) | see | better | like

Vocabulary:

タクシー taxi | より more than | 電車 train | 安い cheap | 本 book | 読む to read | 映画 movie | 見る to see | 好き like

ANSWERS:

1. タクシーより電車のほうが安いです。

2. 本を読むより、映画を見るほうが好きです。

10. 〜が上手です

ABOUT:

■ skilled at; good at

■ Construction:

N + が上手です

V + のが上手です

EXAMPLES:

1. 私の姉は、ピアノが上手です。

2. 彼女は、ギターが上手です。

3. 彼は、歌うのが上手です。(use の with a verb)

EXAMPLE 1

私の姉は、ピアノが上手です。

[my | older sister | as for | piano | skilled]

My older sister is good at piano.

EXAMPLE 2

彼女は、<u>ギター</u>が上手です。

[she | as for | guitar | skilled]

She is good at guitar.

EXAMPLE 3

彼は、<u>歌う</u>のが上手です。

[he | as for | to sing | skilled]

He's good at singing.

MAIN POINTS:

■ When used with a verb, remember to add a の.

PRACTICE:

Using this form, how do you translate the following?

1. She is good at dancing.

2. That actor is good at Japanese.

HINTS

1. she | as for | dance | が | skilled; good at

2. that | actor | は | Japanese language | good at

Vocabulary:

彼女(かのじょ) her; she | ダンス dance | 上手(じょうず) good at | あの that | 俳優(はいゆう) actor; actress | 日本語(にほんご) Japanese language

ANSWERS:

1. 彼女(かのじょ)は、ダンスが上手(じょうず)です。

2. あの俳優(はいゆう)は、日本語(にほんご)が上手(じょうず)です。

11. 〜がへたです

ABOUT:

■ bad at; not skilled

■ Just as with が上手です (skilled at), add a の after verbs

EXAMPLES:

1. 私の兄は、歌うのが下手です。

2. あの俳優は、ダンスが下手です。

3. あの先生は、説明が下手で、何を言っているのか、わからないです。

EXAMPLE 1

私の兄は、歌うのが下手です。

[my | older brother | as for は | to sing | not good at]

My older brother isn't good at singing.

EXAMPLE 2

あの俳優は、<u>ダンス</u>が下手です。

[that | actor | as for は | not good at]

That actor isn't good at dancing.

EXAMPLE 3

あの先生は、<u>説明</u>が下手で、何を言っているの
か、わからないです。

[that | teacher | as for | explanation | bad at | and
| what | saying | (regarding) | don't understand]

That teacher is bad at explaining things, and I don't
understand what he's saying.

MAIN POINTS:

■ When used with a verb, remember to add a の.

PRACTICE:

Using this form, how do you translate the following?
1. My little sister is bad at cooking.
2. My father is bad at English.

HINTS
1. little sister | は | cooking | が | bad at

2. my | father | は | English language | が | bad at

Vocabulary:

妹 little sister | 料理 cooking | 下手 not skilled | 私 の my | 父 father | 英語 English language

ANSWERS:

1. 妹 は、料理が下手です。

2. 私 の父は英語が下手です。

12. N＋がほしい

ABOUT:

■ (I) want

■ This is the last of the words we will cover that requires a が.

EXAMPLES:

1. 水<small>みず</small>がほしいです。

2. おやつがほしいです。

3. 新<small>あたら</small>しいドレスがほしいです。

EXAMPLE 1

水<small>みず</small>がほしいです。

[water | want (uses が)]

I want water.

EXAMPLE 2

<u>おやつ</u>がほしいです。

[snack | want (uses が)]

I want a snack.

EXAMPLE 3

新しい<u>ドレス</u>がほしいです。
<small>あたら</small>

[new | dress | want (uses が)]

I want a new dress.

MAIN POINTS:

■ Just like じょうず (good at) and へた (not good at),
ほしい also uses が after the wanted object.

PRACTICE:

Using this form, how do you translate the following?
1. I want a car.

47

2. I want a good textbook.

HINTS

1. car | が | want

2. good | textbook | が | want

Vocabulary:

車 car| ほしい want | いい good | 教科書 textbook

くるま　　　　　　　　　　　　　　　　　　　　　　　　きょうかしょ

ANSWERS:

1. 車がほしいです。

　くるま

2. いい教科書がほしいです。

　　　きょうかしょ

13. ので

ABOUT:

■ therefore; because of that

■ Construction: place after verbs and -I adjectives. Add a な after -na adjectives and nouns.

■ The reason is given before ので and the resulting action follows.

EXAMPLES:

1. 仕事が終わったので、帰ります。

2. 部屋が散らかってきたので、そうじします。

3. お腹がすいたので、サンドイッチを買いに行きます。

EXAMPLE 1

仕事が終わったので、帰ります。

[work | finished | therefore | return (home)]

Since (I) finished work, I went home.

EXAMPLE 2

部屋が散らかってきたので、そうじします。

[room | (subject marker) | messy | became | therefore | cleaning | to do]

My room became messy so I will clean it up.

EXAMPLE 3

お腹がすいたので、サンドイッチを買いに行きます。

[stomach | emptied | therefore | sandwich | (direct object marker) | in order to buy | to go]

I'm hungry, so I'm going to buy a sandwich.

MAIN POINTS:

■ Add な for -na adjetives and nouns; verbs and -I adjectives are unmodified

■ A ので B – Because of A, B is the resulting action

PRACTICE:

Using this form, how do you translate the following?
1. It's late, so let's go home.
2. I'm thirsty, so I'm going to drink beer.

HINTS
1. late | therefore | let's return

2. throat | が | dry | therefore | beer | を | drink

Vocabulary:

遅い late; slow | ので therefore; so | 帰りましょう let's return | のどがかわいた (I'm) thirsty | ビール beer | 飲みます to drink

ANSWERS:

1. 遅いので、帰りましょう。

2. のどがかわいたので、ビールを飲みます。

14. 〜まえに

ABOUT:

■ before (space or time); in front of (space)

■ Add a の before nouns: 家の前 (in front of the house)

■ Use the plain form for verbs. 行く前に (before (I) go)

EXAMPLES:

1. 勉強する前にアニメを見ます。

2. 試験の前に、よく勉強しました。

3. 私の家の前にコンビニがあります。

EXAMPLE 1

勉強する前にアニメを見ます。

[to study | before | anime | (direct object marker) | to see]

Before I study, I watch anime.

EXAMPLE 2

試験の前に、よく勉強しました。

[test | の (limiter: before what? the test) | much | studied]

Before the test, I studied a lot.

EXAMPLE 3

私の家の前にコンビニがあります。

[my | house | in front of | convenience story | there exists]

There's a convenience store in front of my house.

[Note: this 前に refers to spacial rather than temporal spaces.]

MAIN POINTS:

■ 前に can be used for both time (before something

happens) and space (in front of something).

PRACTICE:

Using this form, how do you translate the following?

1. There's a police box in front of the station.
2. Before coming to Japan, I studied Japanese.

HINTS
1. station | 's | in front of | police box | exists

2. Japan | to | come | before | Japanese language | を | studied

Vocabulary:

駅 (train) station | の of | 前に before | 交番 police box; small police station | あります exist | 日本 Japan に to | 来る to come | 日本語 Japanese language | 勉強しました studied

ANSWERS:

1. 駅の前に交番があります。

2. 日本に来る前に、日本語を勉強しました。

15. 〜つもりです

ABOUT:

■ plan to; intend to

■ Construction: plain form verb + つもりです

EXAMPLES:

1. 来年、日本に帰るつもりです。

2. 今日は、よく勉強するつもりです。

3. 今度の日曜日は、映画に行くつもりです。

EXAMPLE 1

来年、日本に帰るつもりです。

[next year | Japan | to | return | intend to]

I intend to return to Japan next year.

EXAMPLE 2

今日<small>きょう</small>は、よく勉強<small>べんきょう</small>するつもりです。

[as for today | much | study | intend to]

I intend to study a lot today.

EXAMPLE 3

今度<small>こんど</small>の日曜日<small>にちようび</small>は、映画<small>えいが</small>に行<small>い</small>くつもりです。

[next | Sunday | as for | movies | to | go | intend to]

I'm planning to go to the movies this Sunday

MAIN POINTS:

■ 予定<small>よてい</small> is similar pattern. While there is overlap with つもり, つもり shows intent while 予定<small>よてい</small> indicates a plan or something scheduled.

PRACTICE:

Using this form, how do you translate the following?
1. Today, I plan to go out.

2. I intend to take a walk

HINTS

1. today | は | go out | intend

2. go for walk | に | to go | intend

Vocabulary:

今日 today | 出かける to go out | つもり intend; plan to | 散歩に to go for a walk | 行く to go

ANSWERS:

1. 今日は、出かけるつもりです。

2. 散歩に行くつもりです。

16. 〜たり　〜たり

ABOUT:

■ to do such things as ... or ...

■ Used to list multiple items in a non-complete list of activities: such things as ... or ...; the implication is there are other such unspoken activities.

■ This construction is often used only once to represent other common and similar activities or things

■ Construction:

- VERBS / -I ADJ: Simple past + り：食べたり
  (things like eating)

- NOUNS / -na ADJ: Simple past + り：猫だったり
  (things like cats)

EXAMPLES:

1. 昨日は、お酒を飲んだり、カラオケに行ったりして、とても楽しかったです。

2. 赤ちゃんは、泣いたり、笑ったりしていま

す。

3. 毎日、走ったり、歩いたりしたほうがいい
です。

EXAMPLE 1

昨日は、お酒を飲んだり、カラオケに行ったり

して、とても楽しかったです。

[as for yesterday | alcohol | drink | things like |
karoke | to | went | things like | did and | very |
enjoyable | was]

Yesterday, I did things like drinking and going to
karaoke; it was very fun.

EXAMPLE 2

赤ちゃんは、泣いたり、笑ったりしています。

[baby | as for | crying | things like |
smiling/laughing | things like | doing]

Babies do things like crying and laughing.

EXAMPLE 3

毎日、走ったり、歩いたりしたほうがいいです。

[every day | running | things like | walking | things like | better]

It's good to run or walk every day.

MAIN POINTS:

■ Used for non-exhausted lists (there are other unspoken examples

PRACTICE:

Using this form, how do you translate the following?

1. On Sunday, I did things like take a nap or watch TV.

2. At the library, a lot of people do things like read books or study.

HINTS

1. Sunday | は | nap | を | do things | TV | を | did things like seeing

2. library | at | I | は | book | を | do things like reading | do things like studying | to do |

Vocabulary:

日曜日 Sunday | 昼寝 nap | したり do things like | テレビ TV | 見たりしました did things like see | 図書館 library | で at | 私 I; me | 本 book | 読んだり do things like read | 勉強したりします do things like study

ANSWERS:

1. 日曜日は、昼寝をしたり、テレビを見たりしました。

2. 図書館で、私は、本を読んだり、勉強したりします。

17. から～まで

ABOUT:

■ From ~ to ~

■ This form can be used both with time and space.

EXAMPLES:

1. あの店は、朝6時から夜7時まで開いています。 (time example)

2. 家から駅までは１キロです。 (space example)

3. 日本語で１から１０まで数えます。 (number example)

EXAMPLE 1

あの店は、朝6時から夜7時まで開いています。

[that | store | as for | morning | 6 o'clock | from | night | 7 o'clock | until | is open]

That store is open from 6 A.M. to 7 P.M.

EXAMPLE 2

家から駅までは１キロです。

[house | from | (train) station | until | as for | 1 kilometer]

From the house to the station is about a kilometer.

EXAMPLE 3

日本語で１から１０まで数えます。

[Japanese language | in | from one | to ten | able to count]

(I) can count from 1 to 10 in Japanese.

MAIN POINTS:

■ Just like "from" and "until" in English, から・まで can be used with time as well as spaces.

PRACTICE:

Using this form, how do you translate the following?
1. From here to the station is close.
2. The test is from 1 o'clock to 4 o'clock

HINTS
1. here | from | station | until | では | close

2. test | は | 1 o'clock | from | 4 o'clock | until

Vocabulary:

ここから from here | 駅 station | まで until | 近い
close | テスト test | 1時 1 o'clock から from | 4時 4
o'clock

ANSWERS:

1. ここから駅までは近いです。

2. テストは、1時から4時までです。

18. 何か

ABOUT:

■ Something

■ The か shows uncertainty. Other question words are similar: <u>いつ</u>か (someday); <u>どこ</u>か (somewhere); <u>だれ</u>か (someone)

EXAMPLES:

1. 何か食べましょうか？

2. それは、何かわかりますか？

3. 何か買って帰りましょう。

EXAMPLE 1

何か食べましょうか？

[something | let's eat | ?]

Let get something to eat.

EXAMPLE 2

それは、<ruby>何<rt>なに</rt></ruby>かわかりますか？

[as for that | something | understand | ?]

Do you know what that is?

EXAMPLE 3

<ruby>何<rt>なに</rt></ruby>か<ruby>買<rt>か</rt></ruby>って<ruby>帰<rt>かえ</rt></ruby>りましょう。

[something | bought and | let's return]

Let's buy something and go home.

MAIN POINTS:

■ The か shows uncertainty.

PRACTICE:

Using this form, how do you translate the following?
1. Do you want to drink something?
2. I want something.

HINTS

1. something | to drink | ?

2. something | want

Vocabulary:

何_{なに}か something | 飲_のみます to drink | ほしい want

ANSWERS:

1. 何_{なに}か飲_のみますか？

2. 何_{なに}かほしい。

19. だれか

ABOUT:

■ Someone

■ As mentioned in the previous entry, the か shows
uncertainty: **some**one

EXAMPLES:

1. あの人は、だれか知っていますか？

2. だれか助けて！

3. だれか私と一緒に行く人はいませんか？

EXAMPLE 1

あの人は、だれか知っていますか？

[that | person | as for | someone | know | do you]

Does someone know that person?

EXAMPLE 2

だれか助けて！

[someone | help]

Someone help me!

EXAMPLE 3

だれか私と一緒に行く人はいませんか？

[someone | I; me | and | together | to go | person | exists]

Would anyone like to go with me?

MAIN POINTS:

■ The か added to words shows uncertainty: SOMEone

PRACTICE:

Using this form, how do you translate the following?
1. Please ask someone.
2. Someone opened the door.

HINTS

1. someone | to | ask (listen) | please

2. someone | が | door | を | opened

Vocabulary:

だれか someone | に to | 聞いて ask | ください please | ドア door | 開けました opened

ANSWERS:

1. だれかに聞いてください。

2. だれかがドアを開けました。

20. どこか

ABOUT:

■ somewhere

■ Continuing our か examples, どこ (where) + か (some) means an uncertain location.

■ If action is taking place "somewhere," use で: どこかで、食べましょう。 (Let's eat (action) somewhere.)

■ If action is moving to or from "somewhere" or isn't limited to a single location use に: どこかに行きましょう。 (Let's go someplace.)

EXAMPLES:

1. いつも世界のどこかで戦争が起こっています。

2. どこか隠れるところはありませんか？

3. 宝物がこの山の**どこか**にかくしてあるらしい。

EXAMPLE 1

いつも世界の**どこか**で戦争が起こっています。

[always | world | of | somewhere | at | war | is happening]

There's always a war going on somewhere in the world.

EXAMPLE 2

どこか隠れるところはありませんか？

[somewhere | hiding | place | doesn't exist | ?]

Is there someplace (we) can hide?

[Note: this is in the negative as in, "Isn't there a place to hide?"]

EXAMPLE 3

宝物_{たからもの}がこの山_{やま}の**どこか**にかくしてあるらしい。

[treasure | this | mountain | somewhere | hiding | exists | it seems]

It seems that there is treasure hidden somewhere in this mountain.

MAIN POINTS:

■ If action is taking place "somewhere," use で

■ If action is moving to or from "somewhere" or isn't limited to a single location use に:

PRACTICE:

Using this form, how do you translate the following?
1. Do you know of a good restaurant somewhere?
2. Do you know where the teacher is?

HINTS
1. somewhere | good | restaurant | を | don't know | ? (use a negative question to ask politely)

2. teacher | は | somewhere; whereabouts | don't know | ?

Vocabulary:

どこか somewhere; whereabouts | いい good | レストラン restaurant | 知りません don't know | か (question) | 先生 teacher

ANSWERS:

1. **どこか**いいレストランを知りませんか？

2. 先生は**どこか**知りませんか？

21. 何も

ABOUT:

■ nothing

■ Construction: 何^{なに}も + negative verb

EXAMPLES:

1. お店^{みせ}には、何^{なに}も<u>あり</u>ませんでした。

2. 私^{わたし}は、事件^{じけん}については何^{なに}も<u>知^しり</u>ません。

3. 台風^{たいふう}が来^きましたが、何^{なに}も<u>起^おこり</u>ませんでした。

EXAMPLE 1

お店^{みせ}には、何^{なに}も<u>あり</u>ませんでした。

[store | as for in | nothing | exists | was]

There was nothing in the store.

EXAMPLE 2

私は、事件については<u>何も</u>知りません。

[as for me, I | case | regarding | nothing | not know]

I don't know anything about the case.

EXAMPLE 3

台風が来ましたが、<u>何も</u>起こりませんでした。

[typhoon | came | but | nothing | happened | did]

A typhoon came, but nothing happened.

MAIN POINTS:

■ There are other words that use the も to mean "no-":
だれも (no one) どこも (no where); like 何も, it is followed by a negative verb.

PRACTICE:

Using this form, how do you translate the following?

1. I'm not hiding anything.
2. I don`t know anything.

HINTS

1. nothing | not concealing

2. I | は | nothing | don't understand

Vocabulary:

隠して concealing | いません not | 私 I; me |わから

ない don't understand; don't know

ANSWERS:

1. 何も隠していません。

2. 私 は、何もわからない。

22. だれも

ABOUT:

■ no one

■ Construction: だれも + negative verb

EXAMPLES:

1. あの人の正体はだれも知りません。

2. 今日は、会社にだれもいませんでした。

3. だれもいない夜の学校は、こわいです。

EXAMPLE 1

あの人の正体はだれも知りません。

[that | person | true character | as for | no one | knows]

No one knows that person's true identity.

EXAMPLE 2

今日<ruby>今日<rt>きょう</rt></ruby>は、会社<ruby>会社<rt>かいしゃ</rt></ruby>にだれもいませんでした。

[as for today | company | to | no one | not exists | did]

Today, no one was at the office.

EXAMPLE 3

だれもいない夜<ruby>夜<rt>よる</rt></ruby>の学校<ruby>学校<rt>がっこう</rt></ruby>は、こわいです。

[no one | not exist | night | 's | school | scary]

It's scary to go to school at night when no one is around.

MAIN POINTS:

■ If you already know the main question words, spending some time learning how to use the uncertainty suffix か and the "nothing" も suffix can greatly increase your vocabulary.

PRACTICE:

Using this form, how do you translate the following?

1. No one can understand this problem.
2. No one came to the party.

HINTS

1. no one – this – problem – not understand

2. party – to – no one – didn't come

Vocabulary:

だれも no one | この this | 問題 problem; question |
わかりません don't understand | パーティー party |
に to | 来ませんでした didn't come

ANSWERS:

1. だれもこの問題がわかりません。

2. パーティーにだれも来ませんでした。

23. どこにも

ABOUT:

■ Nowhere at all

■ Construction: どこにも + negative verb

■ どこ (where) に (at) も (no) = nowhere

EXAMPLES:

1. 宝物なんてどこにもなかった。

2. トイレットペーパーは、売り切れでどこにもなかったです。

3. ユートピアなんて、世界中どこにもない。

EXAMPLE 1

宝物なんてどこにもなかった。

[treasure | such a thing as | no where | was]

There were no treasure anywhere.

EXAMPLE 2

トイレットペーパーは、<ruby>売<rt>う</rt></ruby>り<ruby>切<rt>き</rt></ruby>れでどこにもなかったです。

[toilet paper | as for | sold out and | no where | didn't exist]

Toilet paper was sold out and no where to be found.

EXAMPLE 3

ユートピアなんて、<ruby>世界中<rt>せかいじゅう</rt></ruby>どこにもない。

[utopia | such a thing as | throughout the world | no where]

Utopia doesn't exist anywhere in the world.

MAIN POINTS:

■ The も adds the "no" to question words

Clay & Yumi Boutwell

PRACTICE:

Using this form, how do you translate the following?
1. I was thirsty, but there was no water.
2. There are no children at all.

HINTS
1. throat | が | dry | but; however | water | が | no where | wasn't
2. children | は | nowhere

Vocabulary:

のどがかわいた (I) thirsty | が but; however | 水 (みず) water | どこにも no where | なかった wasn't | こども children | いない wasn't (living things)

ANSWERS:

1. のどがかわいたが、水(みず)がどこにもなかった です。

2. こどもは、どこにもいない。

24. あまり〜ない

ABOUT:

■ not very much

■ Construction: あまり + negative verb

■ This shows the degree of something isn't very much

■ This is sometimes pronounced as あんまり in conversation.

EXAMPLES:

1. あのお店_{みせ}には、お買_かい得_{どく}品_{ひん}は**あまりない**です。

2. 私_{わたし}は、**あまり**コーヒーは飲_のま**ない**です。

3. きのうは、忙_{いそが}しくて、**あまり**勉_{べん}強_{きょう}できま せんでした。

EXAMPLE 1

あのお店^{みせ}には、お買^かい得品^{とくひん}は**あまりない**です。

[that | store | as for | bargain item | not much | not]

There aren't many bargain items in that store.

EXAMPLE 2

私^{わたし} は、**あまり**コーヒーは飲^のま**ない**です。

[as for me, I | not much | coffee | don't drink]

I don't drink much coffee.

EXAMPLE 3

きのうは、忙^{いそが} しくて、**あまり**勉強^{べんきょう}でき**ませ**ん

でした。

[yesterday | as for | busy and | not much | studying | wasn't able to do]

I was busy yesterday and wasn't able to study much.

MAIN POINTS:

■ This shows the degree of something isn't very much

PRACTICE:

Using this form, how do you translate the following?

1. She doesn't clean much.
2. This ramen isn't very delicious.

HINTS

1. she | は | not much | cleaning | を | doesn't do

2. this | ramen | は | not much | not delicious |

Vocabulary:

彼女<ruby>彼女<rt>かのじょ</rt></ruby> she | あまり not much | 掃除<ruby>掃除<rt>そうじ</rt></ruby> cleaning | しない not do | この this | ラーメン ramen | おいしくない not delicious

ANSWERS:

1. 彼女<ruby>彼女<rt>かのじょ</rt></ruby>は、**あまり**掃除<ruby>掃除<rt>そうじ</rt></ruby>を**しない**です。

2. このラーメンは、**あまり**おいし**くない**です。

25. V + てください

ABOUT:

■ please (do/give) this (for/to) me

■ Construction: て form of verb + ください

■ You probably learned ください as "give me" but with the て form of a verb, it also means, "please do this for me."

EXAMPLES:

1. この問題の答えを教えてください。

2. この画面を見てください。

3. 本を読んでください。

EXAMPLE 1

この問題の答えを教えてください。

[this | problem | 's | answer | (direct object marker) | teach (me) | please]

Please tell me the answer to this problem.

EXAMPLE 2

この画面を見てください。

[this screen | (direct object marker) | see | please]

Please look at this screen.

EXAMPLE 3

本を読んでください。

[book | (direct object marker) | read | please]

Please read a book.

MAIN POINTS:

■ With the て form of a verb, it also means, "please do this for me."

PRACTICE:

Using this form, how do you translate the following?

1. Please drive the car.
2. Please raise your hand.

HINTS

1. car | を | drive | do | please

2. hand | を | raise | please

Vocabulary:

車 (くるま) car | 運転 (うんてん) drive | して do | ください please | 手 (て) hand | あげて raise

ANSWERS:

1. 車 (くるま) を運転 (うんてん) してください。

2. 手 (て) をあげてください。

26. V＋ませんか

ABOUT:

■ wouldn't (you) like to...

■ This is a polite way to ask someone to do something with you using the negative. We have this in English too: "Wouldn't you like to go to the movies?"

EXAMPLES:

1. 一緒に食事に行きませんか？

2. 図書館に行きませんか？

3. コーヒーを飲みませんか？

EXAMPLE 1

一緒に食事に行きませんか？

[together with | meal | for the purpose of | won't go | ?]

Why don't we go eat together?

EXAMPLE 2

図書館に<u>行き</u>ませんか？

[library | to | won't go |?]

Why don't we go to the library?

EXAMPLE 3

コーヒーを<u>飲み</u>ませんか？

[coffee | (direct object marker) | won't drink | ?]

Wouldn't you like to drink coffee?

MAIN POINTS:

■ While this is using a negative form of the verb, it is a polite way to invite someone to do something with you.

PRACTICE:

Using this form, how do you translate the following?

1. Would you like some ramen? [wouldn't eat ramen?]
2. Shall we swim in the pool? [won't swim in the pool?]

HINTS

1. ramen | を | not eat | ?

2. pool | at | not swim | ?

Vocabulary:

ラーメン ramen | 食べませんか wouldn't (you) eat |

プール pool | で at. | 泳ぎませんか wouldn't (you)

swim

ANSWERS:

1. ラーメンを食べませんか？

2. プールで泳ぎませんか？

27. V＋たい

ABOUT:

■ want to do; would like to do; expresses a desire to do something

■ Construction: -masu stem of a verb + たい

■ This is similar to ほしい (to want), but ほしい is used with nouns and 〜たい is used with verbs.

EXAMPLES:

1. なにか食べたいです。

2. どこかに行きたいです。

3. もっと詳しく聞きたいです。

Clay & Yumi Boutwell

EXAMPLE 1

なにか<ruby>食<rt>た</rt></ruby>べたいです。

[something | eat | want to]

I want something to eat.

EXAMPLE 2

どこかに<ruby>行<rt>い</rt></ruby>きたいです。

[somewhere | to | go | want to]

I want to go somewhere.

EXAMPLE 3

もっと<ruby>詳<rt>くわ</rt></ruby>しく<ruby>聞<rt>き</rt></ruby>きたいです。

[more | in detail | listen | want to]

I want to hear the details.

MAIN POINTS:

■ This is similar to ほしい (to want), but ほしい is used

with nouns and 〜たい is used with verbs.

PRACTICE:

Using this form, how do you translate the following?
1. I want to own a cat.
2. I would like to buy a new TV.

HINTS
1. cat | を | want to own

2. new | TV | を | want to buy

Vocabulary:

猫 cat | 飼いたい want to have (a pet); want to own (a pet) | 新しい new | テレビ TV | 買いたい want to buy

ANSWERS:

1. 猫を飼い**たい**です。

2. 新しいテレビを買い**たい**です。

28. V＋ながら

ABOUT:

■ while doing

■ Construction: the -masu stem form of verbs + ながら

■ This is a conjunction that indicates the preceeding and following actions take place at the same time.

■ The phrase that follows ながら is the main clause (action).

EXAMPLES:

1. いつも晩ご飯を<u>食べ</u>ながら、テレビを見ています。

2. 音楽を<u>聞き</u>ながら、勉強します。

3. コーヒーを<u>飲み</u>ながら、仕事をしています。

EXAMPLE 1

いつも晩ご飯を<u>食べ</u>ながら、テレビを見ていま
す。

[always | evening meal | (direct object marker) |
eat | while | TV | (direct object marker) | watching]

I always watch TV while eating dinner.

EXAMPLE 2

音楽を<u>聞き</u>ながら、勉強します。

[music | (direct object marker) | listen | while |
study]

I study while I listen to music.

EXAMPLE 3

コーヒーを<u>飲み</u>ながら、仕事をしています。

[coffee | (direct object marker) | drink | while |
work | (direct object marker) | doing]

I work while drinking coffee.

MAIN POINTS:

■ The main clause is what follows ながら.

PRACTICE:

Using this form, how do you translate the following?
1. I drive while listening to the radio.
2. I talk while taking a walk.

HINTS
1. radio | を | while listening | car | を | to drive

2. while smiling/laughing | talk | を | did

Vocabulary:

ラジオ radio | 聞きながら while listening | 車 car |
運転します to drive | 笑いながら while smiling/while laughing | 話をした spoke

ANSWERS:

1. ラジオを聞き**ながら**、車を運転します。

2. 笑い**ながら**、話をした。

29. になります

ABOUT:

■ will become; will turn into

■ Construction: (object) + になります

EXAMPLES:

1. 私は、将来医者になります。

2. オタマジャクシは、カエルになります。

3. 少年は、りっぱな大人になりました。

EXAMPLE 1

私は、将来医者になります。

[as for me, I | future | doctor | will become]

I'll become a doctor in the future.

EXAMPLE 2

オタマジャクシは、<u>カエル</u>になります。

[tadpole | as for | frog | will become]

A tadpole will become a frog.

EXAMPLE 3

<ruby>少年<rt>しょうねん</rt></ruby>は、りっぱな<u><ruby>大人<rt>おとな</rt></ruby></u>になりました。

[boy | as for | great | adult | became]

The boy is all grown up.

MAIN POINTS:

■ This is the polite form of になる.

PRACTICE:

Using this form, how do you translate the following?
1. This empty lot will become a park.
2. I became friends with him.

HINTS
1. this | empty land | は | park | become

2. he | with | friend | became

Vocabulary:

この this | 空き地 empty lot | 公園 park | になります will become | 彼 he | と with | ともだち friend | になりました became

ANSWERS:

1. この空き地は、公園になります。

2. 彼とともだちになりました。

30. 〜すぎる

ABOUT:

■ too much; do something excessively or be in an excessive state

■ Construction:

Verbs: -masu stem form of verb + すぎる

Adjectives: stem + すぎる

EXAMPLES:

1. あまり<u>食</u>べ**すぎる**と、お腹がいたくなりますよ。

2. <u>太</u>り**すぎる**と、<u>体</u>によくないです。

3. お<u>酒</u>を<u>飲</u>み**すぎる**と、<u>二日酔</u>いになります。

EXAMPLE 1

あまり<ruby>食<rt>た</rt></ruby>べすぎると、お腹がいたくなりますよ。

[too much | eat | too much | and then | stomach | become painful | (emphatic)]

If you eat too much, you'll get sick to your stomach.

EXAMPLE 2

<ruby>太<rt>ふと</rt></ruby>りすぎると、<ruby>体<rt>からだ</rt></ruby>によくないです。

[fat | too much | and then | body | to | not good]

It's not good for your body to get too fat.

EXAMPLE 3

<ruby>お酒<rt>さけ</rt></ruby>を<ruby>飲<rt>の</rt></ruby>みすぎると、<ruby>二日酔<rt>ふつかよ</rt></ruby>いになります。

[alcohol | (direct object marker) | drink | too much | and then | hangover | will become]

If you drink too much alcohol, you will get a hangover.

MAIN POINTS:

■ For when you want to say "too much (of an action)".

PRACTICE:

Using this form, how do you translate the following?
1. My room is too hot.
2. My younger brother plays games too much.

HINTS
1. my | room | は | too hot

2. younger brother | は | game | を | do too much

Vocabulary:

私（わたし）の my | 部屋（へや）room | 暑（あつ）すぎます too hot | 弟（おとうと）younger brother |ゲーム video game |しすぎます do too much [する (plain form) → し (-masu stem) →しすぎます (do too much)]

ANSWERS:

1. 私（わたし）の部屋（へや）は暑（あつ）すぎます。

2. 弟（おとうと）はゲームをしすぎます。

31. にします・にする

ABOUT:

■ decide to do; decide upon

■ Construction:

Noun: (noun) + にします

Verb: (plain form of verb) + こと + にします

EXAMPLES:

1. お昼ご飯は、<u>おそば</u>にします。

2. 明日は、もっと<u>勉強すること</u>にします。

3. 週末は、<u>動物園に行くこと</u>にします。

EXAMPLE 1

お昼ご飯は、<u>おそば</u>にします。

[lunch | as for | soba | to decide]

107

I'll have soba for lunch.

EXAMPLE 2

明日は、もっと勉強することにします。

[tomorrow | as for | more | act of studying | decide to do]

Tomorrow, I'll study harder.

EXAMPLE 3

週末は、動物園に行くことにします。

[weekend | as for | zoo | to | act of going]

I'm going to go to the zoo for the weekend.

MAIN POINTS:

■ The plain form version of this is にする

PRACTICE:

Using this form, how do you translate the following?

1. I decided to watch a movie.
2. I decided to take a nap.

HINTS

1. movie | を | the act of seeing | decided

2. nap | を | act of doing | decided

Vocabulary:

映画 (movie) | を (direct object marker) | 見る to see | こと (nominalizes verbs so they can be used as a noun phrase) | 昼寝をする to take a nap

ANSWERS:

1. 映画を見ることにします。

2. 昼寝をすることにします。

32. くらい・ぐらい

ABOUT:

■ about; approximately

■ Construction: Noun + くらい

EXAMPLES:

1. <ruby>半年<rt>はんとし</rt></ruby>くらいは、どこにも<ruby>出<rt>で</rt></ruby>かけませんでした。

2. <ruby>毎日<rt>まいにち</rt></ruby><u><ruby>8時間<rt>じかん</rt></ruby></u>くらいは、<ruby>寝<rt>ね</rt></ruby>たほうがいいです。

3. このジュースは、<u><ruby>半分<rt>はんぶん</rt></ruby></u>くらいは<ruby>砂糖<rt>さとう</rt></ruby>です。

EXAMPLE 1

<ruby>半年<rt>はんとし</rt></ruby>くらいは、どこにも<ruby>出<rt>で</rt></ruby>かけませんでした。

[half a year | about | as for | no where | didn't go out]

I didn't go out at all for about half a year.

EXAMPLE 2

<ruby>毎日<rt>まいにち</rt></ruby><u><ruby>8時間<rt>じかん</rt></ruby></u>くらいは、<ruby>寝<rt>ね</rt></ruby>たほうがいいです。

[everyday | span of 8 hours | about | as for | sleep | is better]

It is best to sleep about 8 hours every day.

EXAMPLE 3

このジュースは、<u><ruby>半分<rt>はんぶん</rt></ruby></u>くらいは<ruby>砂糖<rt>さとう</rt></ruby>です。

[this | juice | as for | half | about | as for | sugar]

About half of this juice is sugar.

MAIN POINTS:

■ Both くらい and ぐらい are used and mean the same thing.

PRACTICE:

Using this form, how do you translate the following?
　　1.　Everyday, I wake up around 7 in the morning.
　　2.　I'd like to lose about 10 kilograms.

HINTS
　　1.　everyday | morning | 7 o'clock | about | wake up
　　2.　10 kilograms | about | like to lose weight

Vocabulary:

毎日 everyday | 朝 morning | 7時 7 o'clock | くらい about; around | に at | 起きます wake up | 10 キロ 10 kilograms (this could also be kilometers depending on context) | やせたい want to lose weight

ANSWERS:

　　1.　毎日、朝7時くらいに起きます。

　　2.　10 キロくらいやせたいです。

33. どのぐらい

ABOUT:

■ About how long? About how much?

EXAMPLES:

1. ここから東京^{とうきょう}までどのぐらい（のきょり）
   ですか？

2. 東京駅^{とうきょうえき}からディズニーランドまでどのくら
   い（のきょり）ですか？

3. タクシーだとどのくらい（お金^{かね}が）かかり
   ますか？

EXAMPLE 1

ここから東京^{とうきょう}までどのぐらい（のきょり）です

か？

[here | from | Tokyo | until | about how much]

About how far is Tokyo from here?

EXAMPLE 2

東京駅からディズニーランドまで**どのくらい**（の
きょり）ですか？

[Tokyo | (train) station | from | Disneyland | until |
about how much | (in distance)]

About how far is Disneyland from Tokyo station?

EXAMPLE 3

タクシーだと**どのくらい**（お金が）かかります
か？

[taxi | with | about how much | (money) |takes]

By taxi about how much will it cost?

MAIN POINTS:

■ This indicates an approximate amount.

■ The どの is a demonstrative pronoun. Another useful
example is いくらぐらい (about how much?).

PRACTICE:

Using this form, how do you translate the following?

1. About how far is Osaka?
2. Every morning, about how much coffee do you drink?

HINTS

1. Osaka | は | about how much | far | is it?

2. every morning | about how much | coffee | を | drink?

Vocabulary:

大阪 Osaka | どのくらい about how much | 遠い far |
毎朝 every morning | コーヒー coffee | 飲みます to drink

ANSWERS:

1. 大阪はどのくらい遠いですか？

2. 毎朝、どのくらいコーヒーを飲みますか？

34. しか〜ありません

ABOUT:
- nothing but

- Construction:

  NOUN: noun + しかありません

  VERB: plain form of verb + しかありません

EXAMPLES:

1. 引っ越したばかりなので、家には、<u>ふとん</u>しかありません。

2. その国は、<u>戦争する</u>しか生き残る道はありませんでした。

3. 薬がないので、<u>寝ている</u>しかありませんでした。

EXAMPLE 1

引っ越したばかりなので、家には、ふとんしか
ありません。

[moved (houses; location) | just | therefore | house
| as for | futon | only have]

I just moved so, at the house, I only have a futon.

EXAMPLE 2

その国は、戦争するしか生き残る道はありませ
んでした。

[that | country | as for | war | only | survive | way
| didn't exist]

The only way for that country to survive was
through war.

EXAMPLE 3

薬がないので、寝ているしかありませんでし
た。

[medicine | not | therefore | sleeping | only have]

There was no medicine, so I could only stay in bed.

MAIN POINTS:

■ This is another grammar point that, when meaning "nothing but," takes a negative verb.

PRACTICE:

Using this form, how do you translate the following?
1. This store has nothing but expensive things.
2. In order to lose weight, you have to exercise (there's nothing but exercising).

HINTS
1. this | store | in | は | expensive things | nothing but

2. to lose weight | in order to | は | to exercise | nothing but

Vocabulary:

この this | 店 store | に in | 高い expensive | もの thing | しか only ありません nothing (but) | やせる to lose weight | ために in order to | 運動する to exercise

ANSWERS:

1. この店^{みせ}には高^{たか}いもの**しかありません**。

2. やせるためには、運動^{うんどう}する**しかありません**。

Download Link

Please go to this website to download the MP3s for all the Japanese: (There is an exclusive free gift on kanji waiting there too)

http://japanesereaders.com/n5bunkei

As an extra added bonus, here is a coupon **for 10%** off your next order at www.TheJapanShop.com. Just use the coupon:

MATANE

(Just use the above word in CAPITALS; no minimum order amount!)

Thank you for purchasing and reading this book! To contact the authors, please email them at help@thejapanshop.com. See also the wide selection of materials for learning Japanese at www.TheJapanShop.com and the free site for learning Japanese at www.thejapanesepage.com.

Made in the USA
Monee, IL
11 October 2023